Emotionally based
SCHOOL
AVOIDANCE

This guide is a collaboration produced by a psychologist (Claire), young person (Kit), and Kit's mum (Hollie). Kit and Hollie have first-hand experience of school refusal and anxiety, and have provided suggestions and tips that worked for them. We hope you find them helpful!

Written by
DR CLAIRE STUBBS
HOLLIE SZABO (MUM)
KIT SZABO (YOUNG PERSON)

Edited by **Karina Patfield**
Design & Illustrations by **Pen&Pringle**

www.drclairestubbspsychologist.co.uk

Emotionally Based School Avoidance
Produced/Published by Dr Claire Stubbs, Dr Claire Stubbs
Text © Dr Claire Stubbs, Hollie and Kit Szabo
Illustrations © Pen & Pringle, 2024
Designer © Pen & Pringle, 2024
Editor Karina Patfield

First Edition

ISBN: 978-1-3999-9133-9

Dr Claire Stubbs is a Counselling Psychologist with extensive experience in emotional and behavioural difficulties in children and young people including anxiety, depression, panic, OCD, chronically low self-esteem and bereavement.

Using brain science and an Internal Family Systems approach, this book brings a compassionate and intelligent lens to see school refusal as a protective mechanism rather than just acting-out behavior.

www.drclairestubbspsychologist.co.uk

"Students who genuinely feel cared for by their teachers do better at school.

When children feel relationally safe, the learning brain opens wide up. Without felt relational safety, the brain will focus on getting 'safe' rather than learning."

KAREN YOUNG | HEYSIGMUND.COM

FOREWORD

Dr. Claire Stubbs and her co-authors Hollie and Kit Szabo have created an easy-to-read and beautifully illustrated handbook for understanding and supporting children who resist or refuse to go to school.

Using brain science and an Internal Family Systems approach, this guide brings a compassionate and intelligent lens to see school refusal as a protective mechanism rather than just acting-out behavior.

This stance brings both parents and school staff into a collaborative rather than adversarial relationship with the child who is struggling. This in turn helps grown ups get to the deepest source of school refusal with the hope of addressing that concern rather than just battling with symptoms.

Dr. Stubbs is a deeply committed child therapist with an uncanny ability to attune to and welcome all the parts of her little clients and their parents. She contributes to a wider audience by writing this wonderful book.

LISA SPIEGEL, MA LMHC
Author of Internal Family Systems Therapys
with Children

WHO IS THIS BOOKLET FOR?

The information in this booklet will help you as adults give children and pupils the information they need to **understand themselves** and the parts of them that are anxious. It is also a useful resource to support your own resilience.

CONTENTS

Emotionally Based School Avoidance....................12

The Fight, Flight or Freeze response.................18

The frontal lobes....................................22

When you feel anxious................................24

Fight-Flight-Freeze 27

Anxious arousal 28

Using IFS 30

Our protective parts 40

Acknowledging your feelings 42

Parts exercise 46

Anxious parts 47

Being a detective 48

Supporting a panic attack 55

Responding to aggression 56

Supporting suicidal parts 60

Dealing with significant trauma 64

Identifying your own parts 68

Unblending 72

Safe Place technique 74

Grounding techniques ···································· 78

Progressive Muscle Relaxation Script ·············· 88

Traffic light system ···································· 94

Principles that can help ····························· 96

Supportive strategies for
neurodiverse children ······························· 108

Reasons why your child or young person may
be refusing school ··································· 110

Strategies for home ································· 112

Strategies to discuss with school ················ 114

School environment ································· 115

Returning to school ································· 122

Further suggestions for whole
school approaches ·································· 124

Home schooling ···································· 128

Useful resources ··································· 130

Visual timetables ·································· 132

Your notes ··· 134

Emotionally Based School Avoidance

This guide aims to view Emotionally Based School Avoidance (ESBA) through a compassionate psychological lens. Ideas taken from various therapeutic modalities are in no way intended as a replacement for therapy, but can be utilised alongside existing therapies to support children and young people.

Emotionally Based School Avoidance is a complex issue that is stressful for the child, the parent, and the school. The more a child is absent from school, the more difficult it is for them to resume normal school life. If school refusal becomes an ongoing issue, it can negatively impact the child's social and emotional development.

School refusal is, as the name suggests, the refusal by a child to go to school. Some will get as far as the school gate and then be unable to go in; others can't even leave the house. "School refusal isn't just not wanting to go to school; it's an extreme form of anxiety that debilitates the child," explains Kay Mawson, founder of School Refusal Support Services.

"The term 'school refusal' implies a choice, but children are no more able to go into school than you or I would be to jump into a pit of spiders."

Emotionally Based School Avoidance affects 4.8% of children in years 5 and 6, peaking at 14.3% in year 11. It is more common in boys.

For all young people and children, the more their important adults (parents, teachers, and coaches) can help them feel heard, seen, safe, and cared for, the more the children will feel safe enough to ask for help. In turn, this allows them space to take safe risks, to be curious, brave, and to learn and grow. Research clearly shows that students who feel genuinely cared for by their teachers do better at school; this is because when children feel relationally safe, the learning brain opens up. Without that felt sense of relational safety, the brain will focus on 'getting safe' rather than learning.

Behaviour that is attempting to achieve the outcome of not being at school is focused on safety for the child. For decades, we have lived in a culture that perceives distressing or 'deviant' behaviour as needing discipline when, in reality, it's actually the child's only way of expressing that something is wrong and they need your help, or to express that, "I am sad, NOT bad".

Discipline does not motivate. It engenders fear or escalates the need to create safety. This is not just a phenomenon seen in children; the same happens for adults too. When in fear, the learning brain shuts down, making it impossible to absorb information. However, when we feel safe, the brain will surrender safety resources and allow them to feed into curiosity, learning, connecting and growing in all the vibrant ways we know we can.

Symptoms of Emotionally Based School Avoidance

Children who display Emotionally Based School Avoidance may demonstrate a number of different symptoms and protective behaviours.

Children who display ESBA can be holding severe emotional and cognitive stress in the face of attending school. Truancy is the sign of a child trying to express distress or upset in some way. Rebellion has been misunderstood in our culture for years; it is actually a protective behaviour and the child's attempt to express that they don't want to do something. There will be a reason or reasons for this. The child may be shopping or hanging out with friends, yet this is not to be confused with having a good time; they are struggling in some way.

On the day of school, the child or young person will often attempt to get up in the morning, put on their uniform, have breakfast and may even make it to the car or the school drop-off zone. But when it comes to taking those last steps, the fear is triggered and they become angry, defiant or distressed. For neurodivergent children, this results in tactile defensiveness (hypersensitivity to touch), and the activation of their nervous system. These are examples of **fight or flight**: an attempt by the psyche to protect the individual. The nervous system detects threat in six-millionth of a second, and the child experiences a biological and physiological response they have no control over. More on this later.

FIGHT

ANGRY
DEFIANT
DISTRESSED
AGGRESSION

FLIGHT

ANXIETY
PANIC
AVOIDANCE
PERFECTIONISM

EMOTIONALLY BASED SCHOOL AVOIDANCE

Up to 80% of young people struggling to get to school are experiencing some form of anxiety. This could be social anxiety, generalised anxiety, separation anxiety, or connected to an unmet educational need as a result of undiagnosed dyslexia, ADHD, autism, or Pathological Demand Avoidance.

The refusal to go to school is actually the child's way of trying to protect themselves.

Can you imagine if going to work was difficult for some reason? A part of you would probably want to refuse to go, too!

Separation anxiety is, at its core, a fear of being separated from a significant person who is believed to be a comfort, safety zone and support figure. Social anxiety is characterised by a marked fear or anxiety about one or more social situations in which the individual is exposed to possible scrutiny by others. Generalised anxiety, on the other hand, is characterised by excessive worrying about a number of events. The strategies and suggestions in this booklet will support all types of anxiety. If you want to do more specific work around the different types, then suggestions for resources can be found in the resources section.

The Fight, Flight or Freeze Response

You come into the world wired to connect. With your first breath, you embark on a quest to feel safe in your body, in your environments, and in your relationships with others. The autonomic nervous system (located in your spine) is your personal surveillance system, always on guard, asking the question, "Is this safe?". Its goal is to protect you by sensing safety and risk, listening to what is happening in and around your body and in the connections you have to others. This autonomic nervous system is made up of two main branches: the sympathetic and the parasympathetic. It responds to signals and sensations via three pathways, each with a characteristic pattern of response. Through each of these pathways, you react 'in service of survival'.

If you were walking down a dark alley alone at night and the leaves rustled on the ground, your sympathetic nervous system would trigger danger in six-millionth of a second, sending a signal to your brain that you are under threat.

The amygdala, located in the right side of the brain, sends signals to the body when there is danger or threat. It tells the body to stop using up oxygen for breathing and prepares the muscles for running or fighting. It turns off the frontal lobes (the logical, rational part of the brain) when it takes over, therefore there is nobody home in the logical, rational part of the building! Hence, when you are functioning from this state, you actually don't know what you are doing.

The stress hormone, cortisol, is released into the body, which triggers the release of sugar from your liver for fast energy during stress.

The oxygen builds up and your carbon dioxide drops. This makes you feel dizzy and confused. The heart beats faster to get the fuel to where it is needed in your body. It might feel like it's pounding too hard or too fast, but it is okay, even though it doesn't feel like it. It knows what it's doing.

The fuel gets sent to your arms in case they need to fight, and your legs in case they need to run. Your arms and legs might feel tight or wobbly.

The body cools itself down, so it doesn't have to overheat if it needs to run or fight.

The digestive system prepares itself, too. It makes you feel nauseous, which is the body's way of getting rid of what it needs to, in case you need to run.

Your hearing changes. Your system is so tuned to sounds of danger that you may not be able to hear sounds of connection. When you are in this state of arousal, it's hard for you to hear people properly.

The ability to read facial cues is affected, and you can misread cues. Neutral faces can appear angry, and you remain on high alert. An inability to read facial cues means a lack of trust in the setting. Connecting can feel unsafe and you feel like you want to escape and hide.

FLIGHT
CAN LOOK LIKE:

Wanting to escape,
running away,
hard to focus,
fidgeting,
restlessness,
hyperactive,
avoiding

FIGHT
CAN LOOK LIKE:

Yelling, screaming,
using mean words,
hitting, kicking, biting,
throwing, punching,
blaming, defensive,
talking back, making
demands, not taking
responsibility

AND CAN FEEL LIKE:

Irritable, angry,
furious, offended,
aggressive

Anxious,
panicked,
scared,
worried,
overwhelmed

FREEZE
CAN LOOK LIKE:

Mind goes
blank, hard
to think,
isolating self,
not wanting
to talk,
hard to
complete
tasks

AND CAN FEEL LIKE:

Depressed, numb,
bored, apathetic,
helpless, zoned out

This process happens just as quickly when there is a trigger related to school for the child or young person. Fear provokes the fight, flight or freeze response, resulting in anger, running away or avoiding, or even total shutdown and disconnection from the world. These responses are the body and brain's way of protecting the child from danger, and in this instance, school feels like the danger.

HOW AMAZING IS

The frontal lobes are in the left-hand side of the brain and are responsible for logical, rational and reasoning thought-processing. They do not start to form until about the age of seven, and are not fully formed until the young person is at least 14. Therefore, when anxious or stressed, children and young people need us to loan them our rational and logical lobes!

Explain to Children & Young People What's Happening When They Feel Anxious

It can be really useful for children and young people to understand what they are going through, and why they are feeling what they are feeling.

Five important points to communicate to your child:

1 Anxiety is normal. Everyone experiences anxiety at times. For example, it is normal to feel anxious when on a rollercoaster or before a test. Some teens may appreciate some facts about how common anxiety problems are. For example, "Did you know that one in seven children under 18 will suffer from anxiety?"

2 Anxiety is not dangerous. Although anxiety may feel uncomfortable, it doesn't last long, and will eventually decrease! Also, most people cannot tell when you are anxious (except those close to you, such as your parents).

3 Anxiety is adaptive. Anxiety helps you prepare for real danger (such as a bear confronting you in the woods), or for performing at your best (for example, it helps you get ready for a big game or speech). When you experience anxiety, it triggers your 'fight-flight-freeze' response, and prepares your body to defend itself. For instance, your heart beats faster to pump blood to your muscles so you have the energy to run away or fight off danger. When you freeze, you may not be noticed, allowing the danger to pass. This response is also called 'anxious arousal'. Without anxiety, humans would not have survived as a species!

4 Anxiety is your system's way of letting you know that something doesn't feel right. Therefore, if your child is sharing that they feel anxious, and whether this is expressed through fight, flight or freeze, they are trying to let you know something is wrong. On the surface, things may look ok to you, yet something is not ok for your child or young person. Anxiety doesn't just present for no reason. Once you can validate your child's feelings and let them know it is okay to feel whatever they feel, then you create a space for connection, supporting them to open up. Children can only feel settled when they feel safe, and they only feel safe when they perceive an adult can see what they need and lead them.

5 Courage never means 'no anxiety'; it means being able to handle the discomfort of anxiety whilst moving closer to brave. Through the strategies in this document, you are helping your child or young person to understand their anxiety and supporting them to be with it, too. Also, once you can be with your child's feelings and acknowledge them, you help them do the same for themselves.

EMOTIONALLY BASED SCHOOL AVOIDANCE

Imagine you are hiking in the woods, and you come across a bear. What is the first thing you would do? You may run away from the bear, or you may simply freeze. Another reaction is to yell and wave your arms to appear big and scary. There are three ways humans react to danger:

FIGHT, FLEE, OR FREEZE.

When we are anxious, we react in one of these ways, too. We may run away or avoid situations that make us anxious, for example, not wanting to go to school. Or we may freeze, such as when our minds go blank, and we can't think clearly. Or we may fight, get angry and lash out at people. Fear is underneath this response.

Can you think of some ways you may **FIGHT**, want to **RUN AWAY**, or **FREEZE** because of scary feelings?

"Sometimes, when we sense something is dangerous or threatening, we automatically go into a state called '**anxious arousal**'. This can happen when there is a real danger, but also when something simply feels dangerous, or frightening, such as giving a presentation in class, or [give an example of something relevant to your child]. Anxious arousal makes you feel jittery, on edge, and uncomfortable. It may also make it hard to think clearly. This feeling can become overwhelming enough that anxious people stop doing things or going places that make them feel anxious."

DO YOU THINK THIS IS HAPPENING TO YOU?

Using IFS to support us to understand the different parts of our children

The Internal Family Systems therapy model designed by Richard Schwartz posits that you are made up of different parts of yourself. When you go for coffee, for example, a part of you can be questioning, "Am I going to resist the cake?" or "I deserve it". We all are born with parts and have the potential to develop parts as we go through life. For example, you are born with an innate capacity for relationships, yet if they hurt you, you will develop parts of yourself that try to protect you in relationships, by avoiding relationships, or by entering into relationships that are not available.

Parts of you also develop beliefs about yourself and the world around you. In this example, the belief may be, 'Relationships are not safe,' 'People hurt you,' 'I wasn't good enough', or 'I didn't get 10/10 in a maths test; therefore, I can't do maths and there's no point going to lessons'. Parts can show up as an inner voice – things you hear yourselves saying to yourself, or behaviours – things you do or don't do to protect yourself.

The wonderful premise of the IFS model is that it helps you see that all your parts are trying to protect you in some way, by either looking after you with others, or trying to protect you from emotional pain, or painful beliefs that you have developed through your experiences.

Your parts reside in your emotional brain. As children are predominantly emotional brain until the age of seven, and without a fully developed frontal

this is
too much for me

I am overloaded

I am
no good

I feel bad

I feel worthless

I will
fail

no one
understands my
needs at school

people
are mean to me

When children or young people at school, in your home, or in your care in some way, get blended with their frightened parts, you need to lend them your self-energy/ heart.

EMOTIONALLY BASED SCHOOL AVOIDANCE

lobe until the age of 14, you can understand why they can present as 'blended' with their parts. Blended is an IFS term, describing when you feel taken over by these parts, like the clouds blocking the sunshine.

In addition, IFS proposes that we all have an inner wisdom. This is the big heart we are all born with. The IFS model suggests that when you are born, your heart possesses innate qualities that enable you to be calm, curious about the world, confident, compassionate towards yourself and others, eager to connect, creative, caring, and have courage to overcome your challenges. The IFS model describes these eight Cs as aspects of your self-energy, or your heart, if you prefer (we do!). Stressful or traumatic experiences result in the development of 'parts' that your psyche enlists to protect you. These

'parts' can then be like clouds in your system, blocking access to your big heart (the sunshine) or your wise one within.

When children or young people at school, in your home, or in your care in some way, get blended with their frightened parts, you need to lend them your self-energy/heart. This will help the clouds clear so they can feel the sunshine again and access their own inner wisdom. Through your own self-energy, you impart compassionate understanding, help the child get curious about what they are feeling and why, gain clarity as to the issue, and put strategies in place that support their confidence in attending school. This guidance also suggests some creative strategies that support their engagement in school, enabling them to feel safe and connected with nurturing others through this difficult time.

Let's take this back to school and school anxiety with a hypothetical example.

BOY 1   BOY 2

One young boy, let's call him **Boy 1**, is bullying another young boy, let's call him **Boy 2**. Boy 1 is bullied by his parents at home, and he also witnesses them bullying each other. He bullies Boy 2, as does Boy 1's mum, who shouts and berates Boy 2 when she sees him at school.

Parts Development and Impact:

Boy 1: Has a part that has internalised that the way to deal with conflict is to bully the other person. He has a very angry part of him because he has also witnessed and experienced bullying at home. Additionally, he has a part of him that has been hurt by the bullying and has a belief that other people hurt you. He protects himself (without knowing, of course, as he's only a child), by getting angry at others, as anger acts like a shield or bodyguard to feelings

underneath, remember! He also protects himself by trying to control others. That way he believes he won't get hurt as he is in control, having himself been controlled at home. Because he has been criticised A LOT at home, he also has a part of him that will criticise others, and he can be very critical of himself. These parts of him have been internalised from his family, hence the name Internal Family Systems Model.

Boy 2: Has a part that believes, 'I am bad' following the impact of the bullying by both the little boy and the mum on the way to school. He has a part that tries to protect him from feeling like he is bad, by trying to be a 'good' boy ALL the time. And because relationships have been scary, he has a part of him that pleases others to keep other people okay, so they don't shout at him and treat him badly. Can you see the protector parts here? The 'good' boy part believes that, "If I am good, then no one can accuse me of being 'bad' so hopefully I'll be safe in the world now!" Also, the people pleasing part believes that by keeping everyone happy, he won't have to worry that people will be mean to him again, because there is a part that also believes that he is bad and therefore it is his fault he is bullied. Boy 2 lives in a family where he has learned to be kind and nice to others, so he has internalised these parts and doesn't know how to stand up for himself.

Everyone, including the mum in the playground, has internalised parts from their family of origin and is ultimately doing their best to survive. Just because you are an adult, it doesn't necessarily mean you know what you are doing, how you are reacting, or how to do

it differently. Everyone has their story and has internalised parts from their own family, which then guides them as to how to be in the world with others. When trying to understand other people's parts, their parts' stories and their protective behaviour, it's important to stay open-hearted and curious so you can understand, on an individual level, the meaning of their story and their parts.

Recap. We ALL have:

- Multiple parts of us, like sub-personalities.

- These parts hold beliefs, feelings, and physical sensations.

- Some of these beliefs that may show up in the context of school and school anxiety, include, "No one likes me," "I am not good enough," "I am likely to fail," "I cannot do anything," "I am the odd one out," "I am different," "I am bad," and "people are better than me".

- We then try to hide these beliefs away and develop protector parts that behave either by working really hard at school; trying to please others; avoiding going to school; avoiding getting ready in the morning; trying to be perfect; rebelling by not going to school (this feels safer, especially if the child or young person doesn't feel they have anyone to talk to); being ill leading up to going back to school; injuring themselves to avoid school; and so on. Ultimately, as human beings, we are always trying to protect ourselves from feeling difficult beliefs and emotions, so we do what we can to ensure that protection happens.

- Some of these beliefs will be connected to your family of origin. What parts do you notice in the family/your family, and how do people cope with difficulty and protect themselves?

PROTECTOR PARTS

Don't go to school

Stay home and be safe

Don't be you

Be nice to everyone

BELIEFS

Noone likes me

I am bad

I am worthless

I am likely to fail

EMOTIONALLY BASED SCHOOL AVOIDANCE

All your and your child's parts have a story, a reason why they feel, believe and try to protect themselves in the way they do. We all want others to hear our story, including you. Try to open your heart to hearing their story. There will be a section later which will help you separate from your parts so you can be with your child's. Or, if you are reading this and you are a teacher, sometimes your own parts may take over.
The guide on 'unblending' (separating from your own parts) will support you too.

ALL OUR PARTS ARE PROTECTIVE AND HAVE A POSITIVE INTENTION FOR YOU

Some Points for You as Parents, Carers or Teachers:

CHILDREN'S PARTS ARE TRYING TO PROTECT THEMSELVES

They are not trying to make things difficult for you. Parts' reactions are NOT personal even if they feel like it. Honestly, they are just trying to communicate their distress to you!

ANXIETY CANNOT JUST BE 'GOT OVER'...

If only! Anxiety can only be effectively managed by increasing our understanding of it, of why it's shown up, and what it's trying to let us know about what's happening for us. This then increases our tolerance for it, and we can invite in qualities such as compassion, understanding and care for those parts of us. Equally, it allows us to look at what action needs to be taken to address the issue underneath the child's anxiety, too.

OUR CHILDREN'S PARTS TRIGGER OURS

Understanding, mapping out your parts and your triggers is vital. This is true for anyone in a caring role, too.

THE TEMPTATION TO RATIONALISE FEELINGS

Because we have big hearts as parents and ultimately want to support our children to feel better, it can be tempting to try to rationalise away their feelings. "You'll be fine," "It's not that bad". Trying to rationalise fear or convince a child they shouldn't be scared will only drive their feelings underground. When we try to rationalise our children's fears, they hear and feel, "I am not ok for feeling this way," and will try to dismiss their own feelings, potentially escalating the issue, leaving them feeling lonely and frightened. It can even result in them feeling an anxiety about the anxiety, as they internalise that it's not safe to feel this way. Children and young people need less logic and more presence and connection from us. "Tell me more about how you are feeling," shows them that you are sitting alongside them, and you can gain more information about the fear too; where it's come from and what it's really about.

ATTENDING OUR OWN NEEDS

To enable us to be there for our children's parts means that it's crucial we first attend to our own. This is similar to the plane analogy in which we encourage you to put on your oxygen mask first to enable you to care for others. Strategies for you to unblend are further along in the booklet.

WORKING ON OUR OWN FEELINGS AND PARTS

In doing so, we can support our children and young people to trust their feelings, as we want to encourage this in them. The anxiety will be there for valid reasons; you might not understand those reasons, yet they are valid for your child. If we can show them that we trust how they feel, they will internalise that trust and carry it with them through to adulthood. We want them to follow their instincts: "Something is not right here for me, and I need further support".

ANGER, RAGE, REBELLION, TRUANCY

are all protective parts and not to be confused with deviant behaviour. Seeing them through a lens of deviant behaviour means that we miss the distress or upset for the child, which could be more detrimental and escalate the issue.

EVERYONE IS TRYING TO DO THEIR BEST TO SURVIVE

with the knowledge, information and resources they have at any one given moment... including you!

E-MOTIONS ARE CALLED E-MOTIONS

for a reason. They need to be acknowledged and moved through our psyche. The feelings and parts of the child, their parents, and teachers need to be acknowledged, otherwise they build up and shout louder to be heard, or result in overwhelm.

VALIDATE, VALIDATE, VALIDATE!

We all want to be heard and understood, as this validates feelings. Avoiding your feelings may be a part that you have internalised from your family. We live in a society that provides lots of ways to avoid, yet when we avoid, our bodies interpret it as confirmation of danger and it triggers our internal alarm system. The more we push our feelings away to avoid the feeling of distress in our body, the more they spring back up to gain our attention.

ACKNOWLEDGING YOUR FEELINGS
EXERCISE

As alien as this may feel to you, we need to try to invite our feelings in, as if they were sitting next to us on the chair.
Try this exercise.

1 Start by deep breathing. Place your hand where you feel the anxiety, anger, sadness, whatever the feeling.

2 If the feeling feels too intense, gently tell that feeling that you can see it and you want to be with it. Ask it to soften or give you a little space so you can be with it and hear how it feels. Keep deep breathing.

4 See how long you can bear this sensation for. Remember, if you have parts of you that put the brakes on your feelings at other times, those parts will still be inside you to protect you.

3 Ask the part/feeling if it is willing to share a little bit of how it feels with you. Keep repeating the second step if the feeling gets too overwhelming. And remember to breathe deeply. This will keep your frontal lobes online and help you unblend.

Parts exercise

Have a think about your own beliefs and how you might protect yourself. What parts of you stop you from feeling the discomfort of not being good enough? What do you do to protect yourself from feeling this way? What was your school experience like, and what parts of you were developed as a result? How has this experience impacted how you respond to protect your child? Is this part protecting you from your own feelings of the past, or protecting your child from feeling the way you did? Reflecting on your own time at school and the parts of you that came about as a result of school will really help you on your journey of working and supporting your child, or the young person you are caring for or supporting.

When you have parts of you that are anxious, what do you feel you need? What does this tell you about what the child you are supporting or caring for might need?

PHYSICAL FEELINGS

e.g., Tummy ache, headache, heart racing

BEHAVIOURS

e.g., Finding mum, staying home from school

THOUGHTS

e.g., "I am scared of failing"

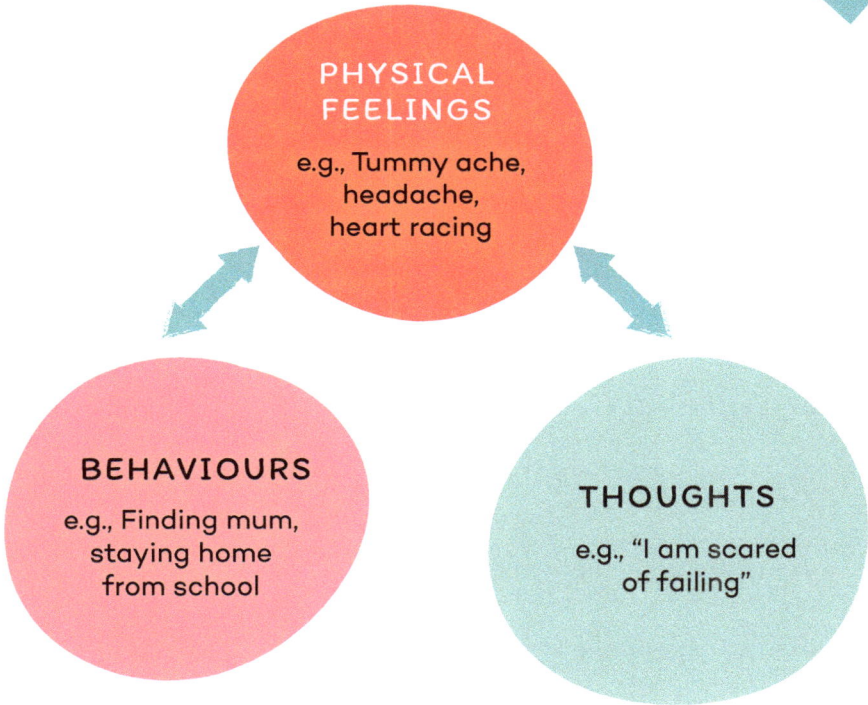

Explain to your child the three parts of anxiety: beliefs or protector parts can show up as thoughts (what we say to ourselves and hear inside), physical feelings (how our body responds), and protective behaviours (what we do, or which actions we put in place to protect ourselves).

Helping your child identify their anxious parts

For younger children, talk about how you will both be 'parts detectives,' and how you will help your child in an 'investigation' to find out more about their anxious parts and the parts story. As detectives, find examples of how your child experiences anxiety in each of the three ways: physical symptoms, how and where the part shows up in the body, what does this part believe about itself? For example, "I am no good," "I am bad," "I will fail," "There is too much to remember," "There are too many things to do". The latter two refer to executive function barriers, in which there is too much auditory information, and the child or young person is unable to process it, as with dyslexic students. What does this part get the person doing? Does it make them avoid lunchtime, make them not want to go to school, make them tell you they are ill, make them hurt themselves prior to school, and so on?

PHYSICAL FEELING DETECTIVE QUESTIONS:

Where do you feel the feelings in your body?

What is the sensation?

Do you feel it anywhere else in your body?

If this feeling were a colour, what colour would it be?

If this feeling were a shape, what shape would it be?

BEING A DETECTIVE

Mapping out anxious parts and where they are in the body.

To help your child recognise physical symptoms, draw a sketch of a body and ask your child to identify where he or she feels anxiety in the body. Prompt your child, if necessary, with an example: "When I feel anxious, I get butterflies in my tummy, and I get a big lump in my throat. What happens when you feel anxious?" Have your child lie down on a large piece of paper (e.g., butcher's paper) and trace his or her body. Teenagers may rather just talk about it or identify their own symptoms whilst talking to you - check with them to see what they prefer. If age-appropriate, ask your child to come up with a name for the part of them that feels anxious (e.g., Mr. Worry, Worry Monster). Refer to your child's anxious part with this new name.

Older children respond well to mapping out their anxious parts too. This also helps with externalising these parts of them, helping them feel separate. Let children be as creative as they want, drawing out their parts or using colours they feel represent the parts of them, using magazine cuttings, clay, or Lego. All these tools help the externalising of parts.

Invite the child or young person to let you know if this part of them has any beliefs about themselves, and things they hear these parts saying to themselves or about others. Provide them with some examples of your beliefs to help them if they are not sure. Ask them, "Where did this part of you get the information?" or "Where did this part learn that they were bad/not important/not good enough/a failure?" This will help you explore the parts' story.

Tip: We (the authors) have learned over the years to just really trust the parts' perception.

You might have seen things differently or have different grown-up knowledge, yet the danger is that this can be dismissive or leave the part feeling overlooked or not heard. Parts have had this experience and drawn this conclusion and therefore need to be witnessed and acknowledged for that upset or hurt. Being curious creates connection as opposed to rationalising. Rationalising can result in a disconnect and the child deciding that their feelings are not okay in some way.

"What does this part or other parts get you doing when you feel no one likes you/you are not important/whatever the belief is?"

This question invites you and the child to begin to understand how they are trying to protect themselves through their behaviour.

"When this part that doesn't feel good enough shows up, what do you do to protect yourself?"
"Are there parts of you that get you doing something to try to protect you from feeling like you've failed?"
"When you feel like you have no friends, what do you find yourself doing to protect yourself from this feeling?"
"How is the part of you that gets you withdrawing from others trying to help you, and then what happens next?"

These questions then lend themselves to mapping out a cycle of protection inside the person as an attempt to keep themselves safe.

Asking the child or young person, "What is this part of you afraid will happen if you go to school?" will also help to elicit the real fears around school and go some way to explaining

the school refusal behaviour. Or you could put it this way, "Is the part of you that wants to keep you at home/ hurts yourself before going to school/gets poorly before going to school/gets really upset on the day of school (whatever the protective behaviour is) afraid what will happen if you go to school?" Once this is understood, then it's easier to start putting things in place to address what is happening, either with the child directly or in partnership with the school, too.

You could then get curious with the child or young person and ask:

"The part of you that feels like they have no friends. Is there anything this part would need to feel a bit safer at school/does that part of you need any help making friends?"

Or leave it really open and ask, "What does that part of you need from us to make attending school a bit safer/easier?"

Or "The part of you that is scared to walk through the playground in the morning, can we do anything to support that part of you to feel a bit safer by coming in a bit later/coming in a different entrance?"

Try to respond to the part of the individual that this curiosity reveals to see what this part would need in order to feel safer. Additionally, validating this part's experience will go a long way to supporting the child to feel safe to open up and share. It's really important to involve the child in the plan to return to school. How can we know what they need if they are not part of the dialogue? This doesn't mean that they need to attend boring adult meetings to discuss it, yet the inclusion of their voice within the meeting is crucial. After all, they will be the one needing to return to school.

These strategies and questions are also helpful for children to see this part of them. You could ask, "Are there any parts of you that feel differently about going to school or have different feelings about school?" If the answer is no, it could be that the child is blended with the fearful part at this point and cannot access any other part of them. It can be really important just to validate this.

These strategies help your child adopt an observer role when dealing with anxiety, giving them a greater sense of choice about how to respond when a part shows up.

We all respond to our parts in ways which protect ourselves. If you wanted to understand more about the child's (and your own) internal response to the parts of them, you could also ask:
"When the anxious part of you shows up, how do you feel towards that part of you?"

If the child responds,
"I get angry towards that part of me,"
that gives you a clue that they are trying to protect themselves by getting angry.

Continuing to be curious would look like:

"I see. What is the angry part angry about?"

"I can understand why the angry part would feel angry."

"What is the part of you that gets angry trying to do for you/ how is it trying to help?"

"What would the angry part be afraid would happen to you if it didn't get angry at you?"

We can be curious with ourselves in the same way. The answers will help us understand how our, and the child's, internal systems are trying to protect themselves during this difficult time.

HOW TO SUPPORT A CHILD WHEN A PANIC ATTACK PART SHOWS UP

If you are at all unsure whether your child is having a panic attack, a heart attack, or an asthma attack, and/or the person is in distress, call an ambulance straight away.

If you are sure that the student is having a panic attack, move them to a quiet, safe place if possible.

Help to calm the child by encouraging slow, relaxed breathing in unison with your own.

Encourage them to breathe in and hold for three seconds and then breathe out for three seconds.

Be a good listener, without judging.

Explain to the child that they are experiencing a panic attack and not something life-threatening, such as a heart attack.

Explain that the attack will soon stop and that they will recover fully.

Assure the child that someone will stay with them and keep them safe until the attack stops.

When we respond to a child through being compassionate, curious, or understanding, we show them how to respond to themselves, too.

Responding to aggressive/ fight parts in our children

As we have highlighted, there are three major nervous system responses to fear: fight, flight, and freeze. More recently, fawn has been added, whereby we submit and try to keep the other safe. We don't want to over-complicate things, so for now we will concentrate on the fight response.

As we have described, when a child or young person is in the 'fight' response, this means their frontal lobe has shut down, the emotional brain has taken over and they feel threatened in some way. To add to this threat and fear, they don't understand what's happening to them and why they are feeling this way. This addition escalates their feelings.

When they are saying, "I hate you," and physically lashing out, they are letting you know that they are not liking how they are feeling, and they are in desperate need of someone to show them protection and help them. Because they are children, and mostly emotional brain, they don't know how to be in this state and articulate what they need. When we see their behaviour through an understanding lens, it helps both with our response and our connection to them. Remember, as we stated earlier, their behaviour is about self-protection and expression. It's NOT personal, or an attempt to make things difficult for you. They are terrified in these moments.

What do they need from you?

Support in keeping them safe. If they are lashing out, they need your help not to do this. You can do this by gently and assertively saying, "I know you are struggling right now, and I also know that you do not want to hit me, so I am going to protect your hands and help you get to a space where we can be calmer." This can be hard for us if we have parts that struggle with authority or challenging behaviour, so this may need to be worked through in the 'identifying your own parts section'. You may encounter challenges as you are trying to stay calm and grounded whilst being on the end of behaviour that triggers early traumatic experiences. Once you are aware what it connects with inside you, then you are in a more informed position when with your child, enabling you to be with them in the present, knowing where their behaviour takes you back to in the past.

Containment, safety, and presence are what they need from you. Contain the situation by:

- Moving them to a calmer, more discreet place if needed.

- Helping them stay safe.

- Stopping any hitting or biting by gently grasping their hands, or wrapping them in a deep bear hug, if their parts will allow.

- Letting them know that you are there with them, alongside them, in this difficult moment.

I AM HERE WITH YOU. I LOVE YOU. YOU ARE HAVING A TOUGH TIME RIGHT NOW AND WE WILL GET THROUGH THIS TOGETHER.

Can you imagine if your partner tried to talk to you about other ways of managing your anger when you are cross at them? This applies to children too. We cannot hear when we are distressed, so any insight into what happened, or learning opportunity will not be gained in this moment. Be aware that additional auditory stimulation, in the form of talking, could make them more aggressive as the listening part of their brain has disconnected.

Supporting suicidal parts

If your child or young person shares that a part of them feels suicidal at the prospect of going to school, then this needs to be taken seriously. The situation has developed to a point at which a part of the child or young person feels like this is the only option to make the difficulty disappear. It may be that the issue has been unaddressed for some time, resulting in a significant degree of suffering and a part of them no longer wanting to be here.

Hearing that your child feels this way will be upsetting, and it is important that you access support for yourself. Accessing your own support is key in enabling you to be as present as possible for your child during this really tough time. If they have opened up to you, this is hopeful, as it indicates a part of them wants support and wants to be heard. Here are some tips that you may find useful:

- Really validate how this part of them feels. Try to be curious with them as to how long this part of them has felt this way

- Let them know that you are sad/sorry that they have been alone with this until now.

- Validate the courage that it has taken for them to share this with you.

- What has led to this part of them feeling this way? (What has happened?)

- How have they kept themselves safe up until this point? This question highlights that even though they may be unaware of their own resources, they do have some, as they have supported themselves to tolerate this feeling.

- What do they need from you? What do they want to happen as a result of sharing this with you? These questions highlight what is needed from you to support their physical safety, facilitate communication, and help them navigate school.

- Prioritising their feelings is paramount; we all need to see that our feelings matter. If there is a local counselling service that they can access, ask them if they would be open to talking to someone. Enquire with your local CAMHS/ mental health service for children and young people regarding an assessment. Let them know that your child has expressed feeling suicidal, as this will highlight the level of risk.

- Explore whether the level of pain and upset that they are feeling might be causing parts of them to want to hurt themselves. Parts that self-harm are trying to keep the enormity of pain away. No one chooses to self-harm unless they are really distressed, and the harsh reality is that it does produce a relaxation effect in the body. Harm to the body: cutting, burning, ingestion of sharp objects, has the same effect as any injury or threat. First, the harm stimulates adrenaline production, resulting in increased energy, focus, feelings of power and control and decreased emotional and body sensation, and then a heightened endorphin release, facilitating a relaxation/analgesic effect.

Both occur quite quickly, providing instant relief to someone who feels terrified and overwhelmed by the level of intensity or disconnection.

- Utilise the questions in the IFS section to explore this part of them, and what this part of them might need from both you and the school to ensure they feel safe.

- Wherever possible, and with the child's consent, it is important to share with the school what is happening, and to think about a plan going forward. It may be that the child cannot return to school at this time, particularly if the suicidal part feels very strong. Explore options for working at home so that work is not disrupted, and try to meet with the school as soon as possible to put a plan in place.

- Whatever has led to your child feeling this way, it's important to consider how the school can support a resolution and create an action plan. This also reinforces to the child that their feelings matter.

- Options may include a reduced timetable, working at home until a suitable plan is in place or, if things have really deteriorated, exploring an alternative school.

WE ALL NEED TO SEE THAT OUR FEELINGS MATTER

Dealing with significant trauma unrelated to the School experience

If your child or young person has experienced a trauma that is not school-related, it has the potential to impact on their focus, leading to emotional overwhelm and difficulty interacting socially. Consequently, navigating school can be really challenging during this time. Imagine trying to attend work when you have experienced a traumatic incident in your life. It adds an extra layer of challenge and complexity that can be overwhelming for a young person who doesn't necessarily understand what is happening to them.

Explore with your child what would offer them the most support. Ask them what they need in place to help make school more manageable. As much as you may have your own anxious parts regarding their achievement, try to remember that if they are emotionally overwhelmed, they are going to struggle to focus and absorb information. Therefore, prioritising their wellbeing at school is paramount.

There may be days when they wake up and cannot contemplate school. Imagine a day when our emotional jugs are really full, then add the challenge of navigating a big busy building filled with five-hundred peers, some of whom might tease you, challenge you, or not understand how or what is going on for you. Can you see why staying at home might feel like a safer option on those days? Meet them where they are emotionally and find out what they need on these days. If we give people a choice, then support them, it empowers them to make that choice.

However, when we feel backed into a corner, we either want the option that is not available or we feel misunderstood, alone, and not heard. Perhaps they need to sleep for a little longer in the morning, then see if they feel that attending in the afternoon is an option. If they really cannot face school, could there be a way for work to be available at home? If you remove those five-hundred peers and all the sensory stimulation that school evokes, is working at home easier? Of course, it's a juggling act, but the more you advocate for your child, the more they feel heard, validated and understood, and the more likely they are to take these steps themselves.

It's essential to work with the school, always with your child's consent, to explore how they can provide support and assistance. Schools have lots of experience and expertise dealing with these challenges. Ask your child who they feel safe with at school, and approach them to discuss a plan.

IMAGINE A DAY WHEN OUR EMOTIONAL JUGS ARE REALLY FULL.

BELOW IS A TESTIMONY FROM A PARENT WHO HAD A CHILD EXPERIENCING PTSD

Dealing with children suffering from PTSD is something no parent can prepare for. Our continual learning as parents whilst children grow up within the family is all we can rely on. It's our internal instinct that leads us to take control, discipline, punish, or continually ask the child, 'WHY?. But all a child wants from a friend, parent or teacher is a calm, non-invasive supporting response. You feel like a new parent with L plates on. You have no idea how to react, but the key is not to. The child needs you now, more than ever, to be patient, calm and to give them as much space as they need, but also to listen without reaction when they want to talk.

The lack of resources in schools and the NHS was very evident, so we chose private one-to-one therapy. It's important to involve someone outside the family/friend network. i.e., someone who the child can feel confident in knowing that whatever is discussed, it stays between child and therapist. With this reassurance, the child agreed.

It's fair to say teachers are tested many times every day with kids trying to push boundaries, but a pause and calm response, and a willingness to listen, will promote the child feeling safe and reduce their chances of losing control.

At the end of each session, I would collect the child and, whilst wanting to ask many questions about the session, I put the child first and simply asked, "You Ok?". Anything more is invasive and, as a parent, we are not qualified to ask or deal with any response. Often, they would go straight to their room and cry themselves to sleep. By being patient and not putting my own feelings first, I and the child slowly formed a new bond where they could, on their terms, open up. Often, whilst at school, they learnt to recognise the anxiety signs that they were about to lose self-control. They would call us for reassurance that all was ok, and communicate with teachers who understood why they were too upset to initially attend the class, but would, at some point, feel safe to re-enter the classroom.

We are not out the other side yet, but our child now has the tools to confide in us and cope with the trauma in a way that does not result in self-harm or deterioration of themselves mentally or physically. The child is now able to manage their emotion far better, which has resulted in them embracing their passion for learning, and focusing positively on their GCSEs and future career.

Therapy is not a 'take a pill' and feel better option. The child had buried trauma from years earlier. They had not confided in anyone for support, and the trauma exploded out of nowhere. The child did not know how to cope with the emotions and felt unable to ask for help, opting for self-harming. It took time to build a relationship and trust with the therapist. The child, over time, realised it was a safe place to let out many difficult emotions in a controlled manner, with the support of the therapist at each step.

Identifying Your Own Parts, as The Caregiver/Teacher/Grown Up

Responding to a school refusal issue can be incredibly stressful for you as a parent, carer, or teacher. It may elicit parts that make you feel like you are not being good enough in dealing with the issue, fearful parts that worry about what will happen to you as a parent if you don't get your child to school, fears around employment if you don't get to work on time as a result of a disrupted morning routine, and so on.

Unless you identify what is happening for you as an adult, it makes it harder to be responsive from a self-energy /open hearted place for your children. It is, therefore, really useful to map out your parts too, and this can be done in the same way we proposed for the children.

Grab some coloured pens and paper and begin mapping your own parts.

WHAT EMOTIONS ARE PROMINENT WITH REGARDS TO THIS PROCESS? ANGER, FEAR, SADNESS, FRUSTRATION, HOPELESSNESS.

↓

DO YOU HEAR YOURSELF SAYING ANYTHING TO YOURSELF ABOUT YOURSELF? (PAINFUL DECISIONS AND BELIEFS).

↓

DO YOU HEAR YOURSELF SAYING ANYTHING ABOUT OTHERS WHO ARE INVOLVED, SCHOOL STAFF, TEACHERS, COLLEAGUES, ETC.?

WHERE DO YOU NOTICE THESE PARTS IN YOUR BODY?

↓

IS THERE A PARTICULAR PART OF YOU THAT SHOWS UP REGULARLY? WHAT DO YOU NOTICE TRIGGERS THIS PART IN YOU? SOMETHING INTERNALLY, OR WHEN SOMETHING HAPPENS EXTERNALLY?

↓

HOW DO YOU RESPOND TO THIS PART OF YOU? DO YOU GET CRITICAL, ANGRY AT YOURSELF? HOW DOES YOUR RESPONSE IMPACT ON HOW YOU FEEL?

↓

HOW IS THIS PART OF YOU TRYING TO PROTECT YOU? WHAT WOULD IT BE AFRAID WOULD HAPPEN IF IT DIDN'T GET ANGRY, CRITICAL AT YOU OR OTHERS?

↓

HOW DOES BEING WITH YOURSELF IN THIS WAY IMPACT YOU?

↓

IS THERE SOMETHING IN YOUR FAMILY OF ORIGIN OR PAST THAT HELPS YOU MAKE SENSE OF THIS RESPONSE THROUGH AN UNDERSTANDING LENS?

Remember, ultimately **YOU ARE DOING YOUR BEST**. You are a good parent/teacher/carer, having a tough time. We all have parts that become reactive, as this is sometimes the only way they know how to respond, or have learned to manage in the past.

If you are reading this and are aware that parts in you have been reactive towards your child throughout this school refusal process, firstly place your hand where you feel that part of you, and send it a clear message that you were doing your best. Anger is a protective part and underneath is often fear, sadness or some kind of vulnerability.

Secondly, it's never too late to repair with your child. Repair can also go a long way to children being able to acknowledge their own reactivity in communication, AND you send them a clear message that your reaction wasn't their fault. It was coming from parts in you that felt frightened or hurt in some way, and you will show your child that you are human and that they are not responsible for how you feel or how you react.

For example:

Child: 'I don't want to go in today.'

Parent: 'You have to go in, or I'll lose my job/get a fine.'

This gives you a sense of the protective parts at play here. For example, verbalising the fears of compromising financial safety/losing the house/ how hard it was to get an understanding boss/ having to stay at home again is exhausting, as the anxiety coming from the child is very demanding. As hard as it may be to trust, as the parent testimonial states, allowing these protectors to step back creates space to be with and validate your child's feelings. This, in turn, makes them feel heard, seen and validated, eventually developing confidence in how they feel.

"As hard as it may be to trust, as the parent testimonial states, allowing these protectors to step back creates space to be with and validate your child's feelings. This, in turn, makes them feel heard, seen and validated, eventually developing confidence in how they feel."

Furthermore, it will create connection between you, as opposed to a disconnection or an escalation of the fear for both of you.

What do your parts need from you around losing your job or getting a fine? Understand that there may not be immediate solutions to these concerns. Placing your hand on your body where you feel these parts, and validating that these concerns are real for you can go a long way to supporting them to unblend. Recognise that these parts in you are looking after you. Let those parts know you will come back to them and attend to those fears later, once you have invested some time in your child.

Once we identify the parts that are at play, then we can practise trying to separate from them, and support ourselves to 'unblend' when we need to.

Unblending

Blending happens when a part takes you over. For example, when all you feel is anger or anxiety. 'Blending' feels similar to when our bodies get triggered into the fight, flight, or freeze response. We have been activated, triggered by something externally that feels threatening in some way to us.

When we are blended, we are not in touch with our inner wisdom, and it can be hard to find clarity, feel confident as a parent, create calm for our children, or connect with our inner courage.

In order to unblend, or to feel separate, it can be really helpful to flesh out what it feels like in your body when a particular part of you takes over. Going back to those physical questions earlier:

Where in your body do you feel the anger/sadness/rage/frustration?

What is the sensation in your body?

What is this part saying to you? Either about yourself or someone else.

What is this part afraid is going to happen to you if you don't respond in this way?

Is there a pattern of thoughts and behaviours when this part of you shows up? (Morning routine, school meetings, when your child gets triggered). Knowing this can help with the planning and unblending.

Now you will have a clearer understanding of what happens when you get blended. Place your hand on where you feel this part of you, breathe in deeply for three seconds, out for three, until your nervous system feels in a calmer place. Then connect in with this part of you and ask:

"Would you separate from me, so that I can look at you and get to know you?" (If this is the part that you are trying to get to know).

"Would you consider stepping back for now and I will return to you later to hear what you have to say?" (If the morning routine is in full flow, for example, and you need to return to a calmer state, it can be helpful for our parts to let them know that you will return to them later).

What does this part need from you to step back? Following this question, our parts often let us know that they need us to connect with them more frequently, to not allow others in the meeting to silence us, to take the pressure off the morning routine so you can be calmer for you and your child. Our systems are very wise and if you ask this question, your part will let you know what it needs from you.

If you are in a school meeting and you notice that you are blended, it is okay to remove yourself and go to the toilet so you can unblend. When you're feeling blended and overwhelmed, you may perceive threat from another person in their tone of voice, or perceive facial expressions that are not there. When you have unblended, rejoin the meeting and ask questions. Now that the wise part of you can fully hear the conversation, it is ok to clarify points you may have missed or misheard. Remember, it is your meeting too, and therefore important that you can feel as present as possible.

SAFE PLACE TECHNIQUE FOR PARTS TO STAY SAFE

Safe place is a concept used in therapy to support people to process difficult experiences whilst soothing their nervous systems via the safe place imagery. Adapted by Joanne Twombly (2022), it can also be used as an internal home for parts to reside when accessing difficult places or times in life, such as going to school. You can also use this for your own parts when attending school meetings or facing situations that feel tough for you.

Before you create your safe place, make sure that:

- You are sitting in a comfortable position.

- You are unlikely to be interrupted.

- You are warm enough. It is useful to have a blanket available as it is common for your temperature to drop when sitting still for any length of time.

If you are able to, it is preferable to close your eyes as this prevents you from being distracted from other visual images. If for any reason you feel unable to close your eyes, rest your gaze where it naturally falls onto the floor in front of you.

Create a safe place in your mind. If it is difficult for you to imagine feeling 100% safe, imagine going to a place where you can feel as safe as your current imagination allows.

Your safe place can be absolutely anything you choose it to be. It could be a place you have been to, or still go to. It can be a place that is totally made up by you, or it can be a combination of both. It can be a place where you are alone, or a place where there are other people of your choosing. Some people opt to have animals with them in their safe place. Anything goes. It is yours and yours alone, and therefore you can make it anything you want it to be.

When you have created your safe place, take time to experience it in as much detail as possible. Use all of your senses to experience your safe place and create a haven for them.

What can you see?
What can you hear?
What can you smell?
What can you touch?
What can you taste?

Remember, your safe place is a place where absolutely nothing/ no one unwanted or uninvited can intrude. Some people find it helpful to create an imaginary force field around their safe place where only that which is wanted or invited can get through.

Pick a word for your safe place so that when you say that word to yourself, it can act as a cue for your safe place. It can be helpful to carry a wallet card with your cue word on it, or more details about your safe place. It can also be useful to have a pictorial representation of your safe place. This could be through using photos, drawing or collage. The cue word, and written detail and/or pictorial representation can be particularly helpful if you need your safe place in an emergency. It can sometimes be difficult to remember important information when you are feeling overwhelmed. For this reason, it is also important to practise going to your safe place in your mind when you don't necessarily feel the need to.

"We need our safe places to be as safe as possible; they are our places."

It could be helpful to give yourself a cue for going to your safe place. Choose something that you do several times a day, for example, going to the loo, or making yourself a warm drink. Use whichever activity you choose as your cue to go to your safe place. For example, if you have chosen making yourself a warm drink, each time you make a warm drink, you go to your safe place. This helps it to become a practised technique, a familiar place which can make it easier for you to use when you really need it, and a habit that your protective part could use.

Once the safe place has been created, check with your child or young person if the part of them that feels afraid would be happy to be there. This might feel strange to you, yet children are so intuitive and mostly embrace these sorts of exercises! If they are not able to be internal or go inside themselves, try to support them to make a safe place using Lego, or sand tray figures, or collages using magazines, or drawing a safe place.

Check with them how safe the place feels and if there is anything that would support it to feel safer for this part of them. See if the anxious/afraid/angry part will tell them what they need in order for it to feel safer here. They can imagine soundproofing the safe place, or it can be a space that is emotion-proof too! Or they may need a safe person there with them, or a pet that is safe. Just let their imagination roll with it and see what they need. Do the same for yourself too! We need our safe places to be as safe as possible; they are our places. It's up to you or the child how it looks, smells, feels and sounds!

Additional grounding techniques

Let's breathe:

START BY BREATHING IN FOR THREE SECONDS,
HOLD YOUR BREATH FOR THREE SECONDS,
AND THEN OUT FOR THREE SECONDS.

HOLDING IN FOR THREE WILL REALLY
SLOW YOUR BREATH DOWN.

EACH BREATH IN NEEDS TO BE INTO THE BELLY AND IDEALLY
FILL UP FOR THE COUNT OF THREE. TO ENSURE YOU BREATHE
INTO YOUR BELLY AND NOT YOUR CHEST, PUT ONE HAND ON
YOUR TUMMY AND ONE HAND ON YOUR CHEST. THE HAND ON
YOUR TUMMY SHOULD MOVE MORE AS YOU BREATHE IN.

THE OUT BREATH SHOULD BE SUSTAINED FOR THE WHOLE
COUNT OF THREE. IMAGINE YOU ARE PULLING YOUR BELLY
BUTTON SLOWLY TOWARDS YOUR SPINE.

Why do this? Breathing deeply and slowly sends a message from your body to your brain that all is well and there is no cause for alarm. It is worth practising so you can use deep breathing when you start to feel anxious. Don't wait until you are in a panic, as this is much less effective.

FURTHER BODY TECHNIQUES

TAKE YOUR SHOES OFF. PLACE BOTH FEET FLAT ON THE FLOOR. FEEL THE TEXTURE OF THE FLOOR ON THE SOLES OF YOUR FEET. NOTICE IF THE FLOOR IS WARM OR COLD.

WIGGLE YOUR TOES. CURL AND UNCURL YOUR TOES SEVERAL TIMES. SPEND A MOMENT NOTICING THE SENSATIONS IN YOUR FEET.

STOMP YOUR FEET ON THE GROUND SEVERAL TIMES. PAY ATTENTION TO THE SENSATIONS IN YOUR FEET AND LEGS AS YOU MAKE CONTACT WITH THE GROUND.

CLENCH YOUR HANDS INTO FISTS, THEN RELEASE THE TENSION. REPEAT THESE TEN TIMES.

PRESS YOUR PALMS TOGETHER. PRESS THEM HARDER AND HOLD THIS POSE FOR 15 SECONDS. PAY ATTENTION TO THE FEELING OF TENSION IN YOUR HANDS AND ARMS.

RUB YOUR PALMS TOGETHER BRISKLY.
NOTICE THE SOUND AND FEELING OF WARMTH.

REACH YOUR HANDS OVER YOUR HEAD LIKE YOU'RE
TRYING TO REACH THE SKY. STRETCH LIKE THIS FOR
FIVE SECONDS. BRING YOUR ARMS DOWN
AND LET THEM RELAX AT YOUR SIDES.

STAND UP AND WALK AROUND. IF YOU ARE IN FREEZE,
THIS WILL DILUTE THE FREEZE.

PAT YOUR ARMS AND LEGS UP AND DOWN — PATTING
ORIENTATES YOU INTO THE PRESENT AND FURTHER
REMINDS YOU OF YOUR PRESENCE IN THE HERE AND NOW.
THIS WILL HELP IF YOU FEEL NUMB OR DETACHED (FREEZE).

TAKE FIVE MORE DEEP BREATHS AND NOTICE
THE FEELING OF CALM IN YOUR BODY.

Breathing exercises are very effective, but they may get a little boring if you are a little person. So, here are a few variations that may be more effective with younger children:

TISSUE BLOWING

Take a tissue and separate the two layers, so you end up with two very thin tissues. Take one of these tissues and throw it in the air. The challenge is to keep the tissue up in the air as long as possible. Keep count of how long your child can keep the tissue in the air and challenge them (in a humorous, gentle way) to improve on their previous effort. This technique has a two-pronged effort because it helps the child refocus and increases their oxygen intake. It can also be lots of fun to do in a classroom setting, as it inevitably leads to people bumping into one another and everyone laughing. What a wonderful way to bring about class cohesion and release tension. If this is very activating for their system, you may need to end the breathwork with deep pressure exercises, such as a weighted object on their lap, pushing themselves up on the chair, or giving themselves a big hug and massaging their own arms.

BUBBLE BLOWING

This is also a lovely way of increasing oxygen into the body, reducing anxiety and redirecting attention.

THE ONE MINUTE RELAX

The one minute relax is a simple and effective technique that combines breathing exercises and Mindfulness practices in a short period. This technique can be ideal for the young person or child to do whilst visiting the bathroom at school, or in the car on the way to school, or you as a parent when you are gearing up for the morning challenge of getting your child to school.
To practise the one minute relax:

FIND YOURSELF A QUIET PLACE TO SIT.

SIT WITH A STRAIGHT BACK AND YOUR HEAD LOOKING STRAIGHT AHEAD.

TURN YOUR PALMS UP ON YOUR LAP, THIS MAKES YOUR SHOULDERS DROP, AND HAVE YOUR FEET FLAT ON THE GROUND.

NOW, SLOWLY CLOSE YOUR EYES AND START CONCENTRATING ON THE AIR GOING IN YOUR NOSE, THROUGH AIR PASSAGES AND DOWN INTO YOUR LUNGS.

YOU MIGHT LIKE TO IMAGINE THAT THE AIR IS

COLOURED
SO THAT
YOU CAN
MORE EASILY
IMAGINE IT
SPREADING
RIGHT DOWN TO
THE BOTTOM OF
YOUR LUNGS AND
THEN BACK OUT AGAIN

IF YOUR MIND WANDERS
— THIS WILL HAPPEN A LOT
WHEN YOU'RE STARTING
— JUST BRING IT BACK TO
YOUR BREATHING.

KEEP YOUR BREATHING
SLOW, DEEP AND
RHYTHMIC, AND CONTINUE
FOR APPROXIMATELY
1 MINUTE.

SLOWLY OPEN YOUR
EYES AND HAVE A
STRETCH, OR SHAKE
YOURSELF OUT,
AND YOU ARE
DONE!

THE HAND ON HEART TECHNIQUE

This is a centring technique that assists with refocusing and de-stressing. It is also beneficial for children and young people with interoception difficulties and who struggle to connect to their internal organs. It not only centres them but also allows them to connect to the sensations in their body. The only downside is that it cannot be done anywhere, at any time. It is more for the morning before school, between lessons, if the pupil is in their quiet area, as they get home from school, or before bed. Like all mindfulness and relaxation techniques, hand on heart calms the body and mind, therefore allowing the brain to release oxytocin.

To practise this breathing technique:

FIND A QUIET PLACE AND SIT WITH YOUR FEET FLAT ON THE GROUND AND YOUR BACK STRAIGHT.

USE YOUR DOMINANT HAND TO FEEL AROUND YOUR CHEST UNTIL YOU CAN FEEL AND HEAR YOUR HEARTBEAT. IT MAY BE FAINT, SO PAY ATTENTION.

ONCE YOU'VE FOUND YOUR HEARTBEAT, CLOSE YOUR EYES AND FOCUS COMPLETELY ON YOUR HEARTBEAT. NOTICE THE DEPTH, TONE, AND SOUND. NOTICE IF THERE ARE ANY DIFFERENCES BETWEEN THE BEATS. NOTICE HOW IT FEELS IN YOUR CHEST.

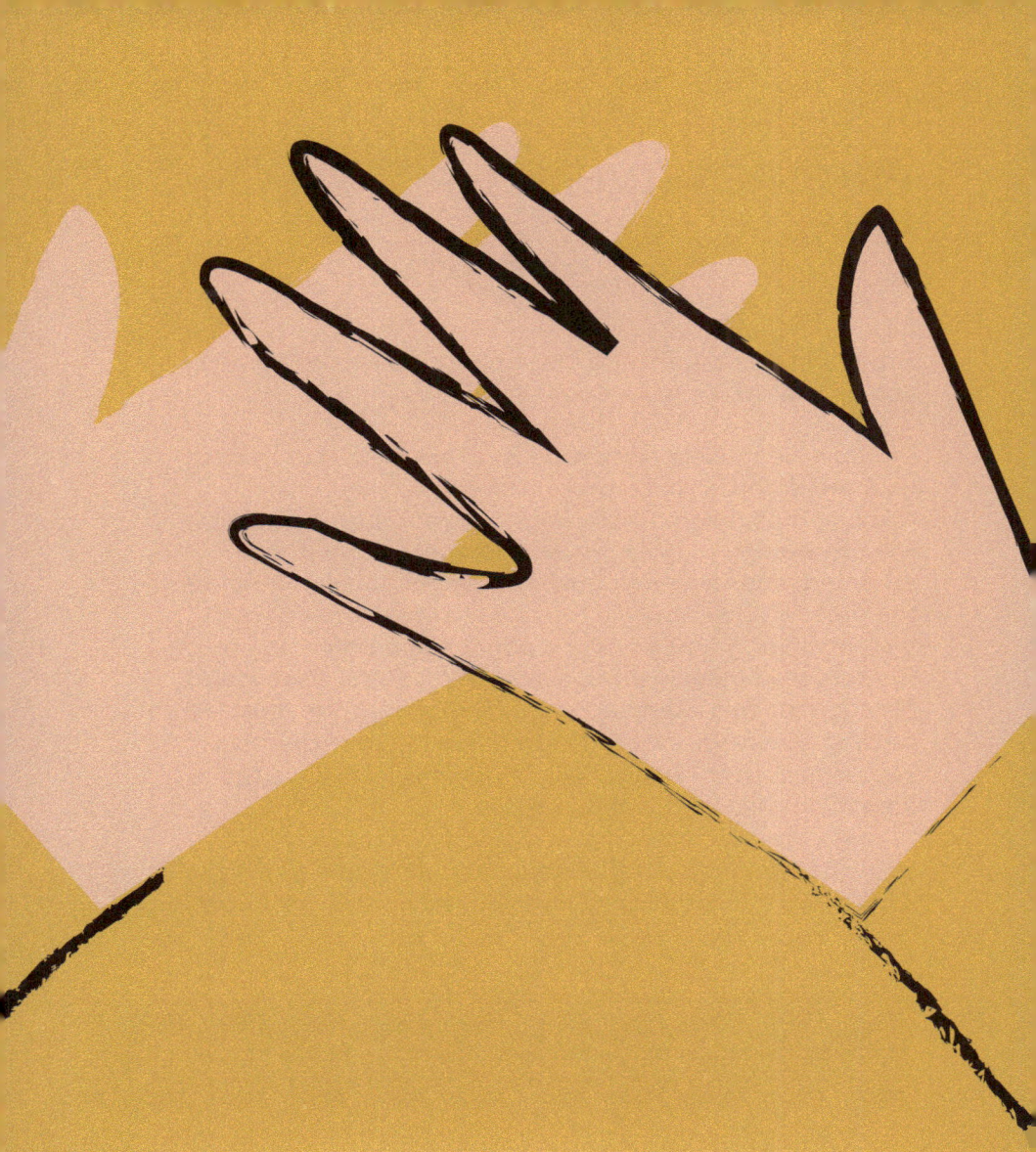

IF YOUR MIND WANDERS, BRING IT BACK TO THE
HEARTBEAT. THROUGHOUT THE EXERCISE, KEEP
YOUR BREATHING DEEP AND RHYTHMIC. DO THIS
FOR TWO TO THREE MINUTES TO START WITH.
INCREASE TO FIVE TO TEN MINUTES AS YOU
BECOME BETTER AT STAYING FOCUSED.

PROGRESSIVE MUSCLE RELAXATION SCRIPT

You might want someone close to you to record this for you as their voice will be soothing, too.

Progressive muscle relaxation is an exercise that relaxes your mind and body by progressively tensing and relaxing muscle groups throughout your entire body. You will tense each muscle group vigorously, but without straining, and then suddenly release the tension and feel the muscle relax. You will tense each muscle for about five seconds. If you have any pain or discomfort in any of the targeted muscle groups, feel free to omit that step. Throughout this exercise, you may visualise the muscles tensing and a wave of relaxation flowing over them as you release that tension. It is important that you keep breathing throughout the exercise.

Begin by finding a comfortable position, either sitting or lying down in a location where you will not be interrupted.

ALLOW YOUR ATTENTION TO FOCUS ONLY ON YOUR BODY. IF YOU NOTICE YOUR MIND WANDERING, BRING IT BACK TO THE MUSCLE YOU ARE WORKING ON.

TAKE A DEEP BREATH THROUGH YOUR ABDOMEN, HOLD FOR A FEW SECONDS, AND EXHALE SLOWLY. AS YOU BREATHE, NOTICE YOUR STOMACH RISING AND YOUR LUNGS FILLING WITH AIR.

AS YOU EXHALE, IMAGINE THE TENSION IN YOUR BODY BEING RELEASED AND FLOWING OUT OF YOUR BODY. AND AGAIN INHALE AND EXHALE. FEEL YOUR BODY RELAXING.

↓

AS YOU GO THROUGH EACH STEP, REMEMBER TO KEEP BREATHING.

↓

TIGHTEN THE MUSCLES IN YOUR FOREHEAD BY RAISING YOUR EYEBROWS AS HIGH AS YOU CAN. HOLD FOR ABOUT FIVE SECONDS. RELEASE ABRUPTLY, FEELING THAT TENSION FALL AWAY.

↓

PAUSE FOR ABOUT TEN SECONDS.

↓

NOW SMILE WIDELY, FEELING YOUR MOUTH AND CHEEKS TENSE. HOLD FOR ABOUT FIVE SECONDS, AND RELEASE, APPRECIATING THE SOFTNESS IN YOUR FACE. PAUSE FOR ABOUT TEN SECONDS.

↓

NEXT, TIGHTEN YOUR EYE MUSCLES BY SQUINTING YOUR EYELIDS TIGHTLY SHUT. HOLD FOR ABOUT FIVE SECONDS, AND RELEASE.

↓

PAUSE FOR ABOUT TEN SECONDS. →

GENTLY PULL YOUR HEAD BACK AS IF TO LOOK AT THE CEILING. HOLD FOR ABOUT FIVE SECONDS, AND RELEASE, FEELING THE TENSION MELTING AWAY.

PAUSE FOR ABOUT TEN SECONDS.

FEEL THE WEIGHT OF YOUR RELAXED HEAD AND NECK SINK.

BREATHE IN... AND OUT. IN... AND OUT.

LET GO OF ALL THE STRESS. BREATHE IN... AND OUT.

NOW, TIGHTLY, BUT WITHOUT STRAINING, CLENCH YOUR FISTS AND HOLD THIS POSITION UNTIL I SAY STOP. HOLD FOR ABOUT FIVE SECONDS, AND RELEASE.

PAUSE FOR ABOUT TEN SECONDS.

NOW, FLEX YOUR BICEPS. FEEL THAT BUILD-UP OF TENSION. YOU MAY EVEN VISUALISE THAT MUSCLE TIGHTENING. HOLD FOR ABOUT FIVE SECONDS, AND RELEASE, ENJOYING THAT FEELING OF LIMPNESS. BREATHE IN... AND OUT.

NOW TIGHTEN YOUR TRICEPS BY EXTENDING YOUR ARMS OUT AND LOCKING YOUR ELBOWS. HOLD FOR ABOUT FIVE SECONDS, AND RELEASE.

PAUSE FOR ABOUT TEN SECONDS.

NOW LIFT YOUR SHOULDERS UP AS IF THEY COULD TOUCH YOUR EARS. HOLD FOR ABOUT FIVE SECONDS, AND QUICKLY RELEASE, FEELING THEIR HEAVINESS. PAUSE FOR ABOUT TEN SECONDS.

TENSE YOUR UPPER BACK BY PULLING YOUR SHOULDERS BACK, TRYING TO MAKE YOUR SHOULDER BLADES TOUCH. HOLD FOR ABOUT FIVE SECONDS, AND RELEASE.

PAUSE FOR ABOUT TEN SECONDS.

TIGHTEN YOUR CHEST BY TAKING A DEEP BREATH IN, HOLD FOR ABOUT FIVE SECONDS, AND EXHALE, BLOWING OUT ALL THE TENSION.

NOW TIGHTEN THE MUSCLES IN YOUR STOMACH BY SUCKING IN. HOLD FOR ABOUT FIVE SECONDS, AND RELEASE. PAUSE FOR ABOUT TEN SECONDS.

GENTLY ARCH YOUR LOWER BACK. HOLD FOR ABOUT FIVE SECONDS, RELAX. PAUSE FOR ABOUT TEN SECONDS.

FEEL THE LIMPNESS IN YOUR UPPER BODY, LETTING GO OF THE TENSION AND STRESS, HOLD FOR ABOUT FIVE SECONDS, AND RELAX.

TIGHTEN YOUR BUTTOCKS. HOLD FOR ABOUT FIVE SECONDS AND RELEASE. IMAGINE YOUR HIPS FALLING LOOSE. PAUSE FOR ABOUT TEN SECONDS.

TIGHTEN YOUR THIGHS BY PRESSING YOUR KNEES TOGETHER, AS IF YOU WERE HOLDING A PENNY BETWEEN THEM. HOLD FOR ABOUT FIVE SECONDS, AND RELEASE. PAUSE FOR ABOUT TEN SECONDS.

NOW FLEX YOUR FEET, PULLING YOUR TOES TOWARDS YOU AND FEELING THE TENSION IN YOUR CALVES. HOLD FOR ABOUT FIVE SECONDS AND RELAX. FEEL THE WEIGHT OF YOUR LEGS SINKING DOWN. PAUSE FOR ABOUT TEN SECONDS.

CURL YOUR TOES UNDER, TENSING YOUR FEET. HOLD FOR ABOUT FIVE SECONDS, RELEASE. PAUSE FOR ABOUT TEN SECONDS.

NOW IMAGINE A WAVE OF RELAXATION SLOWLY SPREADING THROUGH YOUR BODY, BEGINNING AT YOUR HEAD AND GOING ALL THE WAY DOWN TO YOUR FEET.

FEEL THE WEIGHT OF YOUR RELAXED BODY. BREATHE IN... AND OUT... IN... OUT... IN... OUT.

Once you get the hang of this exercise and practise it regularly, it will be easier to respond to the thoughts in your mind. It will also help you drift off to sleep.

TRAFFIC LIGHT SYSTEM

If children struggle to communicate, the
traffic light system can be an alternative
way to let you know how they are doing.
If everyone in the family uses this, it can
be a positive way of understanding where
everyone is at. It is important that everyone
in a household knows how each other is
doing, in terms of managing feelings in
the house. You could have a paper traffic
light on the wall in the kitchen and make
cardboard arrows for each member of the
family. Every day, you place your arrow
where it fits best, in terms of how you
are feeling. I have put examples for the
categories on the traffic light illustration,
yet as a family, it's a good idea that
everyone comes up with descriptors
that are personal to them.

RED

I am really struggling at the moment and terrified of going to school. I cannot remember my strategies as I am in emotion overload and really need help!

AMBER

I am finding things difficult at the moment; I could do with talking through my feelings as otherwise I am scared that my thoughts will get stronger.

GREEN

I am having a good day; I am managing my feelings well and I am feeling positive.

Principles that can help (with all feelings)

PRESENCE

A young woman I was working with once said to me, "I just want someone to sit in the hole with me." Our children and young people really need us to sit alongside them in their struggles, to jump in the hole with them. The learning that comes from this is, "However I feel is ok, and I am not alone in this feeling." This is at the core of confidence building. When we have parts of us that want to rationalise, or help our children see the positive, this is coming from a big-hearted place that wants them to feel better. However, the impact can feel like trying to pull them out of the hole, and the hole will get bigger and feel lonelier. Try, "Tell me more about what leaves a part of you feeling scared about school?", "When did this feeling start?", "What happened that triggered this feeling in you?", "What is it like to feel this way?", and "What can we do together that will support you?"

PATIENCE

Once the anxiety has been identified and a plan put in place, your child's anxious part may show up each morning prior to going to school. If we have had experiences whereby significant others in our lives struggled to sit in the hole with us, it can then trigger parts in us that find it hard to do that for others. Furthermore, when you are in a rush in the morning and someone is not playing ball, it can be incredibly frustrating, and you can panic as you fear that you won't get everything done.

If school refusal is an issue, then wherever possible, it is important to try to make time to support it, so you can be available for your child. This can reduce the pressure around other stressors. Maybe let your boss know this is happening and suggest changes that may need to be put in place – for example, a later arrival. This will allow you to focus on your child and what they need.

There needs to be space to get into the hole in the mornings.

When we are scared, we all need someone to soothe us. This includes YOU. The child's right brain (emotional centre, amygdala) is on overload when they are going through this, so they need you to meet them with your left brain and be soothing, acknowledging their feelings and being supportive. Spending time with your child in this way is not only an investment in their confidence and emotional resilience in the future, but also nurturing a different outcome right now. The tortoise always wins the race! Take the pressure off to create space to breathe and feel — no one is going to be learning if they are in an activated state, so investing the time in the mornings is crucial in support of engagement later in the day.

"I understand how frightened you are, given what has happened previously for you. I can only imagine how hard I would find it going to work. We have spoken to the school and everyone is there to support you and look after you in this."

"I know it is tough for you right now. You are being incredibly brave, and I am really proud of you. What do you need right now from me to support you through this?"

"Ahh, there is Mr Worry, he is trying to tell us something, let that part know that we hear him, and we take on board how he feels, ask the anxious part what he needs from us in order to feel safe today."

Hugging and stroking in the morning will help, alongside the strategies listed and shared in this document. As hard as it is trying to put your frustrations in a box until after 9am, go into the bathroom and use one of the breathing exercises if the stress is overwhelming, or go into the bathroom and curse to let out your frustrations, in a way that your child won't be able to hear. There is a lot of shame already when children are not able to get to school, so hearing your upset at a time when they are vulnerable could add to that shame.

Transitioning after the school holidays also needs to be approached with patience. If your child has a separation anxiety, having six weeks with you and then needing to return to school straight away will be incredibly frightening for those parts of them that want to attach. If you are aware that this is an issue for your child, work with them and the school to see what they would need to support them to feel a bit safer and ease the transition. Try a dry run with them leading up to returning to school, so you can practise how it feels and support your child in mastering their feelings around returning to school. You could take photographs and create a social story that includes positive times. For younger children, this could be read at bedtime, giving their protective parts an outline of the routine and happy memories of the school. The dry run won't escalate the feelings or make the situation worse; it will do the opposite and support you too, helping you to identify what is needed, as well as allowing you to be with your own emerging feelings.

If you have a part that feels frightened that the child is missing school, remember that they won't be able to be present if they are frightened (nervous system and brain section), and therefore learning will be compromised, anyway.

Investing time will support them to return and transition to school in a way that feels manageable and safe. Additionally, you are reinforcing the message that their feelings matter, as well as sitting in that hole with them, holding their hand.

It's really tough being a parent...

...as we have to have one foot in supporting our own nervous systems and the other in with our child it's no wonder we can wobble at times!

PERSISTENCE

You already know this is tough, so this strategy or principle is not about preaching, "Hang on in there," it's about, "What do you need in place so you can persist and hang on in there?" As we have already stated in this guide, looking after you and your parts is crucial.

Psychologists and psychotherapists cannot stress enough the importance of the breathing exercises and meditations we have cited here. These offer something different to connecting with your parts, yet are just as valuable in terms of soothing your nervous system and returning you to a calmer state. This allows you to enjoy life from a different emotional state, and then offer that inner wisdom and heart to your child or young person.

This is a really tough situation, and you will need support. Make sure you have mechanisms in place, like a coffee with a friend after the school run, or another place to offload and share the parts of you that cannot be shared with your child. It is impossible to get through this on your own, so take support when it is offered. If the school is resistant for any reason (and this can happen), don't give up! Your child's education is so important, and they have a right to access one where they feel safe. You know your child better than anyone; hold and trust what you know, and don't allow yourself to be derailed or put off from your mission!

Principles that can help (with all feelings) continued

PLAYFULNESS

This situation can be tough when attending to the different relationships involved: you and you; you and your child; you and your manager; you and your headteacher; you and your partner; you and your child's teacher. Wherever possible, approaching the situation with some playfulness will add light and creativity into the process.

We have mentioned here about getting the pens out, using Lego, clay, toys, etc. to help the child express how they are feeling about this situation, and this also applies to you! We do appreciate this doesn't come easy to everyone, so be kind to yourself in the process. Claire struggles with her creative parts but has been brave, stayed with it, and now actually finds it much easier, yet admits it took courage and persistence!

TOYS

If you have a box of toys, ask the child to bring out the toys that will help them tell you the story of what's happening at school. Or ask them: "Show me with the toys the different parts of you that are having a tough time at school."

LEGO

"Using the Lego, show me what it feels like inside when you go to school or imagine going to school," or, "With the Lego can you tell me the story of being at school, or how frightening it is to go to school?"

CLAY

"Can you show me using the magic clay what parts of you feel like when going to school?" Or just put the clay in the room and see what emerges!

SAND TRAYS

These can be used to illustrate the inner world, using the external figures to answer questions, such as, "Show me what it's like being at school, or when a part of you doesn't want to go to school."

DRAW

You can invite the child to draw a picture of their anxious part and then enquire how they feel towards this part of them. This will give you a sense of their internal response to how they are feeling, as above in the 'mapping out parts' section. Validate, validate, validate!
Paper plates can be great for this exercise too, as they are in the shape of faces, and you can use stickers to add in features.

THE FILL ME UP EXERCISE FROM DR BECKY KENNEDY

In her book Good Inside, Dr Becky Kennedy describes how when children are struggling, they are longing for connection, and need 'filling up' with mummy! She then describes how she says to her son, "I think you need filling up with mummy time" and proceeds to shower her son with cuddles and squeezes! We love this; it has a lovely, playful energy that captures exactly what the child needs.

PERSPECTIVE

This is an incredibly stressful experience and, as we have mentioned throughout, can be triggering for our parts and our nervous system. When we are triggered/ blended, it can be really hard to gain a sense of clarity and perspective. Our hope is that by sharing these tools and activities, the practising and repeating of them, whilst being kind to yourself, will nurture a sense of perspective. This doesn't mean denying what anyone is feeling; quite the opposite, it means being able to hold a helicopter view of the situation, to work out who is involved, what everyone's agenda is, and what needs to happen to support the little person in this process.

Welcoming in all your feelings around this can be a fundamental start. This supports us to be understanding and welcoming of other's feelings too, whilst holding boundaries if necessary. Acceptance is about allowing yourself to accept how you feel about the situation and accepting that your feelings will probably be like a rollercoaster.

For instance, if you have had parts of you that reacted in the morning because your child was aggressive towards you, can you approach yourself with understanding and compassion? As much as we might understand our children's behaviour, it doesn't mean that it's always easy to be on the receiving end of it. When juggling commitments and responsibilities, a challenging morning can be hard to contend with, and we all have parts that react at times. Remember, what matters is the repair for you and your child. You are a super human, yet none of us are superhuman!

Remember, what matters is the repair for you and your child. You are a super human, yet none of us are superhuman!

Accepting how you feel takes out the struggle, because through acceptance, you are acknowledging your own feelings. There will be times when you don't respond how you want to, and that needs to be

okay. Remember, you are human, not a superhero! You will feel angry at times, despairing even, and that is all okay. The more you can accept that these kinds of feelings are normal, the more quickly you will move through them. Judging yourself for your feelings just adds another layer of feeling on top, making them harder to get over.

Try to accept how your child feels too, accepting that this will fluctuate. Remember, they are not choosing to feel this way and, regardless of how the feelings are expressed, they are being driven by fear. Encourage their bravery; we all know how hard it is to do something when we are frightened, so acknowledging this is really important and will be reinforcing for them.

Supportive strategies for neurodiverse children

A special thanks to www.autism.org.uk for supporting this section.

What has been outlined so far is relevant for all children and young people. However, we are mindful that autistic and ADHD children and young people have additional needs that are important to highlight and consider.

Some neurodiverse children cannot attend school because they are unable to cope with the demands of school and the environment. This is sometimes referred to as school refusal, although some individuals feel this terminology implies that the child or young person has a choice when, in fact, they feel unable to attend. School absence or refusal can be ongoing until the reasons behind it have been identified and addressed.

Here we look at reasons that could be behind this. We also suggest strategies to try at home and school to help maintain school attendance, or reintegrate the child or young person back into school.

Neurodiverse children and young people can face additional pressure at school. For example, they may:

- Struggle with the complex social skills that are intuitive to others. They may struggle to establish and maintain friendships, or may experience bullying.

- Experience sensory differences or overload as a result of, for example, the lighting, smells, noise, or the number of people.

- Have difficulty coping with the curriculum. This might be due to challenges in processing information, comprehending questions and text, or the information presented not being dyslexia-friendly. Additionally, dealing with overwhelming auditory information could contribute to these difficulties.

- Struggle to cope with the demands of a school timetable due to difficulty with organisation and prioritising.

- Be striving for perfection in their work and may feel that anything less means they have failed.

- Find transitions, such as moving classroom or changing teacher, and unstructured time, such as breaks and lunchtime, cause anxiety at school.

- Experience difficulty with a particular member of staff or subject.

- Struggle with anxiety and find it hard to be apart from family or away from the familiar routines of home.

Reasons why your child or young person may be refusing school

Explore what your child thinks about their experiences at school. For example, ask how their day has been, but give open options to avoid an ambiguous, "OK" response. Use declarative language, making straightforward statements without asking questions. Visual supports may help. Some children can find direct questions challenging, so try the side door, for example "I used to find going to school hard because of my anxiety about what people were thinking of me." Or use an example that you feel is connected to your child's concerns. By making it about you it normalises the experience whilst making it less threatening.

Useful questions may be

Consider whether there is a pattern to the absences. Are they trying to avoid a particular situation, lesson, or person that causes anxiety?

Speak to a member of staff at school who knows your child well and ask for their help. Your child may be showing signs of anxiety in school at particular times. Alternatively, your child may display different behaviour at home to that in school. Often emotions remain bottled up until the end of the school day, to be released at home where they feel fully loved and accepted.

WHAT WENT WELL TODAY AT SCHOOL?

WHAT WAS THE HIGHLIGHT TODAY?

WHAT SPECIFICALLY DID YOU FIND REALLY CHALLENGING?

WHAT WAS UNEXPECTED? DID ANYTHING GO WELL THAT YOU WERE NOT EXPECTING?

If your child starts to become reluctant to go to school, then it is important to act early, as with any child.

Some of the following may help:

• Encourage your child to communicate with you about the problem. Using visual supports may help. Ask your child to rate events or places at school on a scale from 'not scary' to 'very scary'. Colour-coding can also help. For example, you could create a map or landscape of the school, or a timetable, and ask your child to highlight areas or lessons/teachers/times of day according to emotions. For example, the toilet might be red (angry), and lunchtime orange (wobbly). This may help you see when and where the problems occur and help build your child's resilience.

• Enquire about the parts of them (as above) that find school difficult, and use the questions above to help them map out their parts and explore the parts' anxiety.

• Use visual pictures to help them tell you the story. Comic strips can be effective, allowing the child to draw their day with stick people. This can help them to highlight difficulties and perceptions of conversations.

• Lego, clay and sand trays are great tools for supporting neurodivergent children to share their world.

- If you have an understanding of the reasons behind their barriers to attendance, then share it with school staff.

- Create a worry book for your child to record anxiety during the school day. Rewrite the story with a positive ending, communicating this with the school. For example, if they struggle with PE, their story may include them getting changed and feeling scratchy and itchy, which makes them feel sad for the rest of the day. The ending might change into the child being allowed to wear their PE kit under their uniform, so they don't have to get changed. This makes them feel happy. If appropriate, read the book together as part of their evening routine. You can then help them deal with any worries by suggesting how to cope with them in the future.

- Identify strategies to regulate emotions and reduce stress: for example, exercise, jumping on the trampoline, visual stress scales, such as a stress thermometer or traffic light system, or others suggested in this booklet.

- Provide structure at home by using visual supports that they are part of. There is a daily routine chart at the back of this booklet that you may find useful.

These strategies can be beneficial for all young people and children to consider.

These strategies can be beneficial for all young people and children to consider.

The help your child needs will depend upon the causes of their anxiety. There may be a specific problem which requires immediate action from school. For example, your child may be subject to bullying.

Every child is unique, and it's really important to consider your child's individual needs.

School environment

- Many neurodiverse children and young people have sensory sensitivities. There are specific strategies that can help with this, such as providing a calm and quiet place or a suitable workspace.

- Some children may need seating away from classroom distractions such as doors, windows, cubby areas and pencil sharpeners. Try to limit other distractions in the room, like excessive noise or clutter. Playing brown or white noise can help block out sudden noises, allowing the child's nervous system to feel safe.

- They may need support from an occupational therapist to help identify and manage sensory issues.

- All children need consistency and continuity in their relationships. Continuing to have a dedicated professional supporting them as their secure base at school will be significant in supporting their attachment needs. Someone they know they can go to when they are having a wobble. Perhaps someone they meet in the morning at the gate and is there for them throughout the day.

- A consistent person that meets their need for availability, sensitivity and acceptance. This is not the same as having a full-time tutor. Time must be allocated in the child's day for this relationship, and they will need to know in advance when to expect to spend time with this person.

- Does your child need more or different support at school? Neurodiverse children may need help transitioning between lessons, or may benefit from specialist input from a speech and language therapist to help them understand social situations.

- Visual cues such as timetables are really helpful, so the child knows what is coming next throughout the day/week. Colour-coding school timetables according to subject and emailing them home each week will help children be aware of subjects for a Monday morning. Timetables can also be used to support getting ready in the morning, but remember that it's important that your child has some autonomy over the planning. Tools can be found in the back of this booklet.

- Neurodiverse children can be more sensitive to sensory overload, and a school environment can be really challenging on a sensory level. They may need sensory breaks throughout the day, a quiet space where they can have some downtime to reboot and regulate how they are feeling alongside a supportive other. This is linked to the needs of their sensory system. Is their system seeking activation, alertness, and movement to maintain a feeling of safety, or is it activated and needing deep pressure and proprioceptive input to soothe it?

- An Occupational Therapist can assess your child's sensory needs and prescribe a 'sensory diet' for them at home and school. This will support them in developing the sensory integration necessary to manage the experiences they currently find challenging.

- Use the understanding you have of your child to identify coping strategies that can be used in school and discuss them with the person responsible for special educational needs and disabilities (SEND) or additional support needs (ASN). This could be something like time out cards, stress scales or other interventions. The SENDCo will be able to track the use of the time out card, to see if there are patterns linked to emotional overwhelm.

- Explore if there is a local ISEND (Inclusion, Special Educational Needs and Disabilities service) within your local authority which could help identify your and the child's needs at school.

- Ask the school to make reasonable adjustments at the start and end of the school day. For example, being met at the school entrance by a member of staff your child feels comfortable with, having time to engage in their own hobby/interest, or letting them leave before other pupils.

- Ask the school to consider extra breaks during the course of the school day. Some pupils may need to be redirected to a different activity, have a quick run outside, or retreat to a quieter area of the school.

- Your child may find it beneficial if they are given the opportunity to discuss their feelings at the end of each school day. Ask your child's teacher or support assistant if they could go through the timetable with them, and ask the child to give a mark out of ten for each lesson. For lessons they score low, ask them why.

- Suggest to the school that they use your child's interest to help them learn. Interests can be used to differentiate work so that it motivates your child.

Neurodiverse children can sometimes struggle with their executive functioning. Executive functioning skills, such as task initiation, problem solving, planning, time management, emotional regulation and self-awareness, are vital for getting through the school day.

Other ways we can support the development of children's executive functioning are:

SCAFFOLDING AND BREAKING DOWN TASKS INTO REALLY SMALL CHUNKS.

DEVELOPING CHECKLISTS SO THEY CAN SEE THEIR PROGRESS: "HAVE YOU LOOKED AT YOUR LIST?" "WHAT DO WE NEED TO DO FIRST?"

SLOWLY GIVING INSTRUCTIONS AND REPEATING THEM, SO THEY HAVE TIME TO DIGEST THEM.

RECAPPING AND CLARIFYING ANY EXPECTATIONS.

TRYING TO TAKE ACCOUNT OF ANY EXECUTIVE FUNCTIONING SKILLS THEY MIGHT NEED EXTRA SUPERVISION AND SUPPORT WITH.

TALKING THROUGH ACTIVITIES OUT LOUD.

PROVIDING OPPORTUNITIES FOR MULTI-SENSORY LEARNING (VISUAL, AUDITORY, KINESTHETIC).

GIVING THE CHILD A PRINTOUT OF THE LESSON, SO THEY CAN USE HIGHLIGHTERS AND MAKE THEIR OWN NOTES. OFFERING DYSLEXIA-FRIENDLY LEARNING MATERIALS, INCLUDING APPROPRIATE FONT STYLES, TEXT SIZES, AND SPACING. MORE INFORMATION CAN BE FOUND ON THE BRITISH DYSLEXIA FEDERATION.

When supporting your child to go back to school after a period of absence, it may help to start off on a part-time timetable, with them attending for a short period and gradually building up. This can be better than putting pressure on your child to attend for a whole day and them not coping. The child will have a good sense of what they can manage and what feels safe. Even if the distress is so high that they only commit to an hour, that is a great start.

Returning to school

We should try to work together to identify and address sources of stress, aiming to reduce anxiety levels so the pupil can re-engage with their education by feeling safe in the classroom and accepted by those who support them.

Any period of transition, including returning to school, can cause anxiety, so careful preparation will be needed to help the pupil manage this change.

Involve the pupil in the reintegration process and arrangements, including details that might seem trivial.

For example, which room they will go to first, what time, how long for, what for, and what happens next? A visual timetable may help (see at the back of this booklet).

Before the pupil can access learning, work may need to be done on their emotional wellbeing, reducing stress, and increasing self-confidence. The techniques in this booklet may support this, as they will increase their confidence to deal with their anxiety in the first instance.

WORKING TOGETHER TO IDENTIFY AND ADDRESS SOURCES OF STRESS

- Have a meeting where everyone is involved: parents, the young person, and the school support lead, to identify the difficulties in school, and what support the young person needs to access at school when they are feeling this way.

- Intervene as quickly as possible. If the child feels immediately heard and responded to then re-integration is more likely. Also, there is less impact if the issue is addressed promptly.

- Ensure a clear plan is in place to support re-integration that involves everyone, most importantly the young person or child. If they cannot articulate this or feel too anxious to attend, is there a creative way their views can be heard through a Pupil Voice?

- Ensure the plan is manageable for the young person. Initially, it may be things like just getting to school and standing outside (this can be emotionally evocative enough) or sitting in the library and working. Remember to take it at the child's pace, hear what level of anxiety they are operating at and how much they feel their internal system can tolerate.

- Provide opportunities to work collaboratively with parents and the young person, creating policies, procedures, and training that puts the voice of the child at its heart.

- Support all children, as a whole school approach, in developing self-soothing/grounding activities.

- Validate, validate, validate. Ensure everyone is aware and supportive of the child or young person.

- If parents and the young person or child are so frazzled and burnt out by the issue, then extra support may be required.

- Create a mentor within the school who the young person can go to when they feel this way, and who will provide the information they need to support them.

- Provide information to the young person about thought patterns when they worry, and how they can challenge these.

- Assist the young person and their peers by fostering wellbeing ambassadors who can initiate a school-wide campaign addressing concerns, enabling young people to gain knowledge and serve as advocates for supporting their peers.

- Run a workshop for parents on anxiety and worry, led by the wellbeing ambassadors. See Get Self Help for useful resources to support these. www.getselfhelp.co.uk

- Create an anonymous feedback mechanism within the school for young people to share how they are feeling, especially during times of transition from primary to secondary school.

Further suggestions for whole school approaches continued

- Ensure everyone in the staff team is aware and can check in with this young person, through acknowledging them in the corridor or in class.

- Consider finding another young person in the year group who you could enlist to provide support.

- Use emotional scales throughout the school, providing an inclusive approach to wellbeing. The traffic light system can be really useful in the classroom, at breaktime, and during school trips.

- Arrange for the school's Wellbeing Ambassadors to run assemblies on anxiety, outlining what support is available in the school. Link this to a Pupil Voice that asks everyone in the school how they feel.

Take these ideas and run small projects, communicating them to families through newsletters and parent consultations.

- What support do young people have access to? Are there any clubs at school they could get involved with?

- When organising a school trip for the year, provide families with a comprehensive trip overview, which includes social stories, visuals, and a day schedule, well in advance. This proactive approach will alleviate potential anxiety associated with unfamiliar surroundings. If a child or young person is too anxious to attend a school trip, provide an alternative that is accessible to them.

- Explore outside groups and clubs. Could they access these? What support might they need to physically get there? Consider if the school could provide this.

- Teach skills that encourage their sense of bravery, such as those listed in this booklet.

- Run a tutor group session on this issue and generate ideas from other young people about how they would approach this. (See Centre for Clinical Interventions: www.cci.health.wa.gov.au)

Home schooling

In some cases, if the anxiety is too severe, home schooling may need to be considered. This is where parents assume overall responsibility for the planning, implementation, and assessment of their child's education. The Government legislates a key number of learning areas that need to be incorporated into any home schooling programme, as well as systems to ensure correct use. Home schooling comes with its own set of challenges that this booklet doesn't have the space to do justice to and also tests your resilience as a parent. Another important consideration is your capacity to keep your child motivated, on task, and making academic progress in line with their peers.

HOME SCHOOLING

Useful resources

BOOKS

Internal Family Systems Therapy with Children.
Lisa Spiegel

Good Inside: A practical guide to becoming the parent you want to be.
Dr Becky Kennedy

Helping Children with Complex Needs Bounce Back: Resilient Therapy.
Angie Hart and Kim Aumann

Can I Tell you about Anxiety? A guide for friends, family, and professionals.
Lucy Willetts and Polly Waite

A Short Introduction to Helping Young People Manage Anxiety.
Carol Fitzpatrick

Overcoming School Refusal.
A practical guide for teachers, counsellors, caseworkers and parents, Joanne Garfi.

WEBSITES

www.schoolrefusal.co.uk
This site has a number of useful links and suggested reading.

www.anxietyuk.org.uk

www.autism.org.uk
This website is particularly useful for young people or children with autism.

www.notinfineschool.co.uk
A great resource for families with children experiencing school attendance barriers. There is a great Facebook community which is very supportive too.

www.childtherapyservice.org.uk
A not-for-profit social enterprise that creates evidenced-based resources, training, and support services to improve every child's emotional health.

www.additudemag.com
Range of resources for ADHD

www.chadd.org.uk
For families and children suffering with ADHD.

www.getselfhelp.co.uk
CBT resources on anxiety

www.cci.health.wa.gov.au
Self Help Resources for Mental Health Difficulties

www.ifs-institute.com
For everything Internal Family Systems

www.goodinside.com
Dr Becky Kennedy offers a range of nurturing and supportive resources for parents and deeply feeling kids that everyone can benefit from

www.heysigmund.com
Karen Young has a range of training opportunities and wonderful books that support adults & children to approach anxiety in ways echoed within this resource.

www.boingboing.org.uk
Great resources for children, families, schools with a particular focus on inequalities and social justice

FACEBOOK GROUPS AND PAGES

With Parents In Mind

At Peace Parents: For Children with PDA

Dr Becky at Good Inside

Karen Young Hey Sigmund

Not Fine In School- Public Page- School Attendance Difficulties

Very Special Tales : Clara has lots of wonderful resources

Wholehearted School Counselling

Child Therapy Service

Peaceful Parenting of Kids with Hidden Disabilities

Kids and Teens Psychology

Confident Kids and Teens

Sarah Fisher Connective Family

With You In Mind

IFS Self-Led Parenting Group

IFS Parts Work In Play

Parts and IFS Therapists

IFS with Children and Parents

Visual timetables

Visual timetables can be a brilliant support and help to reduce anxiety by showing what is going to happen in the day. Visual timetables can also aid pupils to be as independent as possible, by visually showing them where they need to go or what they will be doing next.

SO WHAT EXACTLY IS A VISUAL TIMETABLE?

A visual timetable is a schedule that uses objects, pictures or symbols to help children see what is going to happen over the course of a morning, afternoon, day or even a single activity. It can be very simple with a **Now** and **Then** box and a selection of visual symbols to represent the child's activities.

To make your own, you can find visual timetable images at **www.twinkl.co.uk/resources/class-management/daily-routine/visual-timetable**

See visual timetable example overleaf.

WHAT AM I DOING TODAY?

NOW

Register

NEXT

Class Assembly

Class Assembly

Register

Break time

Play

Literacy

PE

Useful notes